Growing Up
Holy
and
Alone

ALSO BY ADAM LEVON BROWN

Death is not our Holy Word
Embedded Memories of a Shooting Star
Angelic Hymns of a Life Once Burdened
Klonopin Meets Sisyphus
Break

©2020 Adam Levon Brown

book design and layout: SpiNDec, Port Saint Lucie, FL
cover image: *Pocketful of Dreams*, silver gelatin lithprint 2006, Kris Haggblom

All rights reserved.

No part of this book may be used or reproduced in any manner whatsoever without written permission except in the case of brief quotations embodied in critical articles and reviews. Members of educational institutions and organizations wishing to photocopy any of the work for classroom use, or authors, artists and publishers who would like to obtain permission for any material in the work, should contact the publisher.

Printed in the United States of America.
Published by Poetic Justice Books
Port Saint Lucie, Florida
www.poeticjusticebooks.com

ISBN: 978-1-950433-25-4

FIRST EDITION
10 9 8 7 6 5 4 3 2 1

Growing Up
Holy
and
Alone

by
Adam Levon Brown

Poetic Justice Books
Port St. Lucie, Florida

dedication

contents

I Watched   3
The Ending   5
Of a Friend   7
And Every Time I Sleep 11
I Hear the Heavens 14
Scorching My Heart 15
And I'll Never Forget 20
The Day I Became 22
Holy 24
And Alone 27

Growing Up
Holy
and
Alone

I Watched

The sign
of my grief
open its wings
to me

I grasp
its hellos
with fist
of bramble,

shaking
the thorns off
from my psyche

My lust
to dig
them
into my hands
to imitate
stigmata
ceases

I spare
them
their fate
and leave
them to sting
me another day

Adam Levon Brown

I shush the
sonnet night, singing
misery to sleep

The imperfect
stem of my
faith, broken
one more time

The Ending

Became the moment
you cried at the finger painting
I did in Kindergarten

I hoped it would never pass

The moment you apologized
for being a bad friend in 3rd grade
and we cried together

I hoped it would never pass

The moment you told me you loved
me more than life itself

I hoped it would never pass

The moment in High school
you told me that if you died,
I should carry your ashes
around my neck

I hoped it would never pass

The moment you cried
on the phone would be
the last conversation
we would have

Adam Levon Brown

The vehicle shrouded
in the mist of rain that
night almost took both of us

I hoped you would never pass

These memories between friends
will never leave me

Of a Friend

Who
guided me
to school
for the first time
though I couldn't
tie my shoelaces

I kissed his cheek
the first time I met him
though I couldn't find my lips

There were bullies
and there were
the words, "Faggot" and "Fairy"
hurled at us like hunters
hoping for open season

I didn't know where
I was going at that age,
just that I was traveling fast

The schoolyard fights
turned into the fight
for my life

The toys I used
to play with now
resemble knives

My joy ended
and turned
into fever rage

My friend
became the
safety button
I pushed to defend
myself

I didn't know
where I was going
at that age, just
that I was
traveling fast

My friend
became
the chainsaw
and I became
the blade

I grew from there,
cutting down
willow trees
to carry on my back,
though I was the only
one weeping

The trees turned
into my legs,
and now I can't grow

I used to laugh
at lumberjacks
for their beards

but now my hair
is the only thing
I have left to hide
behind

I didn't know
where I was going
at that age, just
that I was traveling fast

My friend
held me
together
while
the Heavens
took a break

He crashed
his car one
day, caught
between himself
and his ego

Adam Levon Brown

We were together in the vehicle
though his seatbelt wasn't on

We crashed into a stone pillar
and his life flew from my
plentiful hands to God

I lifted him
with the thoughts of the savior
in my heart and healing in my hands
though the bleeding
failed to stop

My fingers in vigorous
rapture with his face, helped
soothe the inevitable death

I don't know where
I'm going at this age
I just know that I'm
traveling fast.

He died that night,
with so many miles
between us left uncharted

My only closure
being the memories
we shared

And Every Time I Sleep

I hear his voice
clinging to my dreams

He speaks
of the dreams,
the hopes, the bed
we once shared

The fall
from lost
silence
speaks
to me

The pain is an avenue
I don't ever want to see again

I see blood dripping from the
side street sign, it calls
his name to me, even while
I'm awake

The fall
from lost
silence
speaks
to me

Adam Levon Brown

His screams
begging for mercy
that still sting
of scorn and helplessness

And the eventual
silence that crumbled
my heart

The fall
from lost
silence
speaks
to me

I walked away
from my life
that day

And no matter
how many
cars I see
resembling his

The fall
from lost
silence

speaks
to me

And
I know they will crash-
I know they will-
I know they-
I know

I Hear the Heavens

Crash his cheek
against mine

Where/tears/leave/heartache/truly/begins

The sentience of your memory lives
through the wave that chose him for me

Where/air/breathes/water/can/live

The tsunami silences
grasped my brilliance
and pummeled me home

Where/mending/breaks/healing/begins

I would have told him
that I loved him,
but the blue crush
of my heart
had already broken

.

Scorching My Heart

Joel, you saved my life
during a dark period in my childhood

I was so close to suicide,
I could only remember your voice

When you entered my room that day,
a sound jumped into my ear,

It was your voice,

talking me down
from the roof of my mouth
which wept only one word,

"Suicide"

Something collided into my ear,

It was your voice,

crashing the automobile
of my bumper-spinning mind,
which consumed itself in only one word,

"Death"

Adam Levon Brown

Something cried in my ear,

It was your voice,

the baby carriage
I once inhabited was gone,
and I am still here,

though it sits under
the mobile spinning
only one word around in my eyes,

"End"

There was then music
playing into my ear,

It was your voice,

holding the record player
of my eardrum close to your heart,
while I considered only one word,

"Escape"

Something rattled
in my ear,

It was your voice,

holding the bottle
of pills I had planned
to swallow
while I ruminated
on only one word,

"Deceased"

Something whispered into my ear,

It was your voice,

reminding me of all the best
times we had together,
all the lunches,

how you taught me how to tie my shoes,
how you taught me to ride a bike,
how you always reminded me to put
on my coat before going outside,
worrying about me being cold,

Reminding
me of the days spent collapsing fears
with your words of guidance
and your ear of wisdom.

Your whisper changed that one word,
it changed it into danger signs
assembled en masse across every street
corner of my mind,
while reciting only one word,

"Friends"

Your whisper changed that one word,

it changed
it into looking at skyscrapers
from the ground up, turning
them into monuments of freedom,
while reciting only one word,

"Friends"

Your whisper changed that one word,

it changed it into a yearning
to have a child and a hope that this baby
will never have to face
the mobile which once haunted me,
while reciting only one word,

"Friends"

Your whisper changed that one word,

it changed it into a symphony
played between us in open light,

while we laughed
with no tears hidden
there to hold us down,
while reciting only one word,

"Friends"

Your whisper changed that one word,

it changed into a pharmacy,
where medication

became the savior and
not the enemy
to loathe and distrust,
while reciting only one word,

"Friends"

I Knew I was gay
and I wanted to end my life

Your whisper-
Your whisper changed it all

And I'll Never Forget

Growing up in
            the
     hands
        of the specter
that was your love

Leaves
     no smiles
behind

                And when
                      you are seen
                              as different
as other
        as queer

       Loneliness
            tears the moon
                    down to see
                         you fail

Do I call on God
         to ease my pain?

Or do I flagellate
         behind friendly doors
                  to ache closer to him?

I'm holding his hand
                like any other day,
                            though his lips
                                          speak of night instead

I kiss them
                          tenderly, lest
                                  I crash into him
                                          with velvet sincerity

                When the silence
                        becomes your truth,
                                you often forget
                          that the sounds
                    can themselves be wounds

They come
        as scorn
                dressed
                      in the light
of hallelujahs

                        turning the words
     you bite
the Sun for

into the slurs

which harbor
                              your crucifix

Adam Levon Brown

The Day I Became

The obsessive thoughts of
three inches of Polyester missing

The same three inches
that would have changed
my world

Joel, you chose not to wear
your seatbelt, fighting
advice from your family and friends

Three inches of polyester
missing, the crunch
of metal on stone

Before I became

A hungry tooth
made to be extracted

The day I became

A silent sinner
made to repent

The day I became

A flashing flame
to be snuffed

The day I became

A crashing car
A crashing car

A crashing car
A crashing car

A crashing car
A crashing car

And because of you
I'll never forget to fasten my seatbelt

I'll
never
forget
to
fasten
my
seatbelt

Three inches
of Polyester
missing

And now I'm alone

Holy

You were my home
for years before the car
accident stole you from me

The mental abuse I give
to myself, rests
on your loss

The seconds
slow and the
heartbeats begin

I've counted and it takes
two cycles to remember
my love for you

It has been four cycles today,
and it's only 10 A.M.

The seconds
slow and the
heartbeats begin

Abuse, the etymology
being "away" and "use,"

I have stayed away from use,
though with the memories
of your kindness, I still use away

The seconds
slow and the
heartbeats begin

Where do birds fly
when the nest is on fire?

Do they who stay behind
huddle for warmth, or simply burn along
with the memories of home?

The seconds
slow and the
heartbeats begin

Running from past lies
can only bring scrapes
to the heart,
the fall from trust

oh, the sweet,
sweet blood

Adam Levon Brown

The seconds
slow and the
heartbeats begin

Why do lies seek
to bruise bones,
when already
the truth eats
our hearts?

Where there were
five seconds
to count the three
syllables of your name,
there is now only one

The heartbeats
stop and the
naming begins

The last syllable
is caught in my throat, tied
to the last second, choking
on the ashes of my home

And Alone

To be
     alone
is to
     live
         in a place

But not
    in the
        people
            living
                there

      And when you/sift through/the remains
of your life/You will find truth/even when it's not there
      Leaking through/Thread Cobwebs of fate/trapped epicenter
explosions of guilt/shutter light-snapped/camera lens death
      In third person/60 FPS/High-resolution grief stains
Cellophane rapture/we found/ brevity a nuisance
      And decided/ to search on/we signaled with no breath
Eyes seeing/ hallelujah spires/cold brilliance shone
      The final picture/was taken/saved to my Polaroid brain
Look for me/on Polaris/he told me once
      We will always/fade/but never die

    I watched
    the ending

      of a friend

And every
time I sleep,
I hear the

      Heavens
      scorching
      my heart

And I'll never
forget the day

I became
holy and alone

Adam Levon Brown is an Award-winning, internationally published poet, Mental health advocate/sufferer, and cat lover. He is the author of six poetry books. He has had his work translated in Spanish, Albanian, Arabic, and Afrikaans. Boasting over 350 published poems, you can find his writing at such publications as Burningword, Epigraph, and The Good Men Project.

Brown is founder, owner, and editor-in-chief of Madness Muse Press, a literary publishing press dedicated to enacting social change through the power of writing. He also volunteers as part of the social media team for the Oregon Poetry Association.

www.ingramcontent.com/pod-product-compliance
Lightning Source LLC
Chambersburg PA
CBHW080636130526
44591CB00047B/2713